and also to the Greeks
Volume 2: Evangelizing Hope

and also to the Greeks
Volume 2: Evangelizing Hope

*"Testifying both to Jews **and also to the Greeks**,*
repentance toward God,
and faith toward our Lord Jesus Christ"
(Acts 20:21, King James Version)

Dr. Peter Vourliotis

And Also to the Greeks, Volume 2: Evangelizing Hope
© 2021 by Dr. Peter Vourliotis

All rights reserved. No part of this book may be reproduced or transmitted in any form or by any means, electronic or mechanical, including photocopying, recording, or any information storage and retrieval system, except in the case of brief passages embodied in critical reviews or articles, without permission from Dr. Peter Vourliotis: pv@greeksforchrist.org

ISBN: 978-1-7369703-2-4

Printed in the United States of America

Cover & Interior Design by Rick Lindholtz for On the Tracks Media

On the Tracks Media, LLC
onthetracksmedia.com

Table of Contents

DEDICATION

YOU WON'T LAST 1

PREACHING WITH SIGNS FOLLOWING 7

MISSION GREECE..13

GREEK HOUR OF HOPE BROADCAST 19

THE CIRCLE OF MISSIONS..27

GOD WANTS ALL TO BE SAVED......................................33

THE PROPHETIC LEADING 39

DEDICATION

To a servant who loved people and music, my second oldest brother John.

My Brother John served as co-pastor with Vasili Kotsafti for some 20 years in the Church they started in Peristeri, Athens. Each time I went to Greece, I was invited to minister there. John was always on the piano. I was looking to minister and then enjoy a meal with all their people. Next to John was always his loving wife Mary. Niko and Katerina, their children, made their family complete.

John had welcomed me in Paris, on my way to Bible School in Belgium. We were invited by a French family for dinner, and John who sat to my right would explain how to use the fork and knife, and how to eat the appetizer escargot. He was in France studying at the famous Schola Cantorum of Paris for his music education and simultaneously the French language and literature at The Sorbonne.

He was born April 8, 1942. In 1956, at 14, he was leading the choir in his Church, while studying music in Athens. After graduating in France as a pianist and a choir conductor, John returned to Greece, to serve in the army as an officer, to get a job and fall in love with Mary.

In 1966, at 24, John organized "The Society of Friends of Religious Music" and "The Mixed Choir of Religious Music" which for 45 years blessed countless audiences with the message of Jesus Christ through music. The choir ministered to all denominations in Greece, Europe and Canada. They also blessed our Greek Hour of Hope Broadcast audience where they were often our guests as we loved listening to their singing.

John loved people and music. The disciple of love, wrote in 1 John 4:16 & 19, "the one who abides in love abides in God, and God abides in him, …. and… We love Him because He first loved us." John was called to forever abide with God who loved him so much on August 20, 2020.

YOU WON'T LAST | 1

"You won't last more than six months."

That's the welcome I received from someone I revered.

The year was 1969 and for the past 38 years the Church had 37 pastors! So, the old-timer minister was speaking from experience in a Church whose pastors served only for a few months, a year or the maximum two years. It was also my youth he was looking at, 24 years of age and still attending College in my final year. At the end of the six months, the same person told me, "Now you are ready to go preach in Greece." I followed his advice in August of 1973.

My previous seven years had prepared me for this assignment. Visiting and ministering in churches in Belgium, my short pastoral experience in France, and those in Switzerland, The Netherlands and Greece, were all a preparation for the ministry I was asked to do in the church of Oakland. But I was depending upon God, always praying for all things, for all needs and for the sermons I was preaching. And, God was with me in all that I was doing.

Soon, I found myself surrounded by seasoned workers, full of wisdom and of many years with the Lord. From them I learned valuable lessons, as they helped me with much joy in the ministry.

There was Rev. George Samartzis, in his eighties and my assistant. Brother George, as we would call him, was a faithful pastor and elder to the Oakland Church for many years, and was given a room upstairs for his living quarters.

Then, there was Rev. Harry Mamalis, a pioneer missionary to Greece who established churches there, now retired and who lived in an assisted living facility in Oakland near the Church.

Also, there were George and Rev. Georgia Zakedis always ready to teach Sunday School and lead Friday meetings, and Rev. Cameron Holland who was a mature minister and became my new assistant.

Rev. Holland was instrumental in helping me in my ministry to the Greeks, and who taught people about tithing. He was a generous man who offered me to rent from him a one room living-quarters in his property for a minimum rent. I lived there for several years.

When I was asked to be the pastor, the Church had many young people, most of them a little younger than me. So, I became their pastor and also youth pastor.

I started youth meetings and devised a series of lessons on various subjects and a program for young people.

Then, I prayed that God will provide me with someone to help me. God answered my prayer by preparing my brother Theo's heart to come from England. While waiting for Theo to come, I was able to bring in youth pastors. The first of them was a young lady who had just visited Greece and had fallen in love with her people. She became my secretary and our youth pastor. Pamela Sciotto still serves the Greeks for Christ ministry today with her husband Joe from their home in Oregon.

The first several years of my pastorship were a constant revival with signs and wonders taking place in the church. The church was full of people hungry to learn God's word. People were saved, others were healed, baptized in water and/or the Holy Spirit. Lives were changed among the young people. Some of them are now leaders in the Greek Ministry. And, there were miracles among the new families that came from the old country.

Although most of the young people made commitments to Jesus Christ, there were those whose parents stopped them from answering God's call. Those who answered the call of God, however, were blessed and continue to be a blessing.

George Argyropoulos, for example, saved by God's grace, is today my associate. Theodore Babbes and Steven Kizanis, who grew among the Greek Youth, as we used to call the group of our young people then. Now they are happily married with godly families and running their real estate business in the area successfully. There are also many young people that I remember now, Ted, Rita and Thom Babbes, Steve Kizanis, Doreen, Diane and Jonathan Argyropoulos, Dora, George and Tassoula Argyropoulos, Alexandra and Barbie Argyropoulos, Lori and John McClain, Julie, Terry and Leland Kalem, Paul, Kristine and

Janette Melcher, George and Pamela Nickolopoulos, George, Effie and Mary Argyropoulos, George and Kathie Zakedis, Tom Vournas to mention just a few who grew among the Greek Youth. There is also George Nickolopoulos, whom I used to pick up for Sunday School every Sunday morning. He accompanied me to most of the evangelistic outreaches I took in several states. George is now married with Pamela and they have three grown children committed to the Lord and all of them serving God in our church. He loves the Lord and the church with all his heart, and is a successful businessman with a famous restaurant called VAL's in the city of Hayward, and a strong influence in the community. George always says "had the Pastor not stopped by my house to pick me up for Sunday School every Sunday, I wouldn't be with God now."

But not only youths close-by. There are also young people from across the nation like Connie Lillas and Christos Sarantopoulos of Washington State, Paul Zarkas in Texas, the Souris children of Oregon, the Kountouris children in Colorado, the Mentis children in Arizona, the Palassis children of Ohio, the Tsioukas children from Pennsylvania, and many others in different parts of the Country who have now lovely families and serve the Lord faithfully.

I had asked the church to buy me a used car to drive from Bethany College in Santa Cruz to Oakland, a 70 miles distance, in my last semester of school. The Church decided to buy me a used car for $150. But one of our members was not happy with this decision, and set out to cause trouble. I brought this need before the Lord in prayer. That very week I learned that both this brother and his wife had their cars smashed while they were driving, ending up in the hospital. This is how the Lord solved this problem. Of course, I visited both of them in the hospital and prayed for them.

"These things command and teach. Let no one despise your youth, but be an example to the believers in word, in conduct, in love, in spirit, in faith, in purity." (1 Timothy 4:11-12)

PREACHING WITH SIGNS FOLLOWING | 2

As a young pastor, I longed for someone to listen to my plans and what I was praying for the church without any reservation. I found it in Daniel.

I loved to visit Daniel at his machine shop, located at the end of 35th Avenue, not far from the Church's address on 36th Avenue. I would go there not just to sign checks and discuss our church's finances, but because I had found a friend who would listen and offer kind and encouraging words to a 24-year-old young pastor.

Daniel continued faithfully as our Church's treasurer for nearly 40 years, until his hand could no longer write. He was also a silent builder of the Church. Every Sunday morning, he would collect and drive to Church in his Oldsmobile four Georges; George G., George D., George B. and another George.

Daniel was married to Effie, who when she was visiting from Greece, she saw in a vision her future husband, who was Daniel. Effie was a great cook of Greek and American dishes, and soon she was named hostess of the church.

Effie was praying for her brothers who were in Greece, to come and know the Lord. She also had a heart for those who were hungry and in need of a home. One time she told me, "Pastor, when I see someone in need my heart aches."

So, their home was always busy with great dinners and socialization.

Effie brought three of her brothers and their families to America, and of course they were all invited to our church.

One of the families after coming to America decided to try our church for one Sunday, from an obligation they felt they had toward Effie. During the service, the mother felt the presence of God, and said to her family, "this will be our church, we'll come here every Sunday." In fact, the mother and her three children opened their hearts to the Lord Jesus on that first Sunday, and the Father did the same on a later date.

One Sunday, one of the teenage daughters told us that she had a growth inside her mouth that she was told it may be cancerous. Immediately, I anointed her with oil and placing my hand on her, I prayed for her healing. Then, I listen to myself telling her that the Lord had healed her. The following Sunday she testified that she had an examination done during the week and the doctor found nothing wrong with her.

Another man whom Effie brought from Greece decided to sit in the back of the church near the exit, for he could not go without a cigarette for longer than 10 minutes. Effie and other family members who were sitting at the other side of the pews, were looking at him during the service expecting him to exit for a cigarette smoke soon and wondering why he did not. When the service was over and he exited the church with the rest of the people, he pulled the cigarette pack, look at it for a moment and crushed it. He had no longer a craving for cigarettes. God had worked in his heart too.

But the biggest challenge for Effie was to see her own son coming to Christ.

Been a musician, her son had gravitated to the wrong crowd of people, and Effie was praying for him. I remember Effie's prayer at one of our Friday meetings. She prayed in the power of the Holy Spirit for her son's salvation that made a strong impression on me. Her son, came back to God in a wonderful way and had a beautiful salvation experience to go on and be a blessing in the service of the Lord.

In those days I visited hospitals often and prayed for sick people. One of our members who went often to hospitals asked if I can visit someone who was there from Greece and who spoke only Greek. I went to the hospital to visit this person who had "jumped ship," and talked to him about his heart and his need of Christ. He accepted the Lord but there was something about him I didn't quite understand.

Later on, this man, who became a member of our Church and married one of our young women, told me what happened that day when I visited him. "Pastor, when you walked in my hospital room and approached me presenting me with the gospel, I felt a great force coming out of you that pushed me against the wall. I got the impression that you had great powers, that you were a holy man. That's why I rushed to accept the Lord."

Also, there was Peggy. She was one of those members who liked to sing certain choruses and she always was happy in the Lord. Peggy had seen in a vision the house that they were going to purchase. Her husband and two children were happy in their new house until this happened. Peggy's doctor told her that a biopsy had revealed that she had cancer of the uterus and she needed to have surgery as soon as possible. Peggy called me to tell me what the doctor had said and I asked her if she would agree to have a prayer meeting before the surgery in her house. She accepted.

Then, I called our people on the phone, inviting them to come to the meeting on that Friday and if they could also fast. The response was amazing. I remember there were some 60 people in Peggy's house that evening. We began by singing a few songs and taught a short message from the Word of God. Then I invited Peggy to come in the middle of her spacious living-room so I can pray for her. I lay my hands on her and pray in an atmosphere charged with the thick presence of the Holy Spirit. When I finished praying, Peggy started to sing full of joy, for the Lord had done a wonderful work on her. He had lifted a great load from Peggy that was weighted down on her back.

The following week Peggy went for surgery, and the doctor who did the surgery found nothing in the place where the cancer was. Then, the doctor told her that she was lucky for he had found nothing and the only thing that the doctor could say was "Peggy, you are very lucky; Peggy, you are very lucky."

And, as in Acts, chapter 2 says;

"And they continued steadfastly in the apostles' doctrine and fellowship...and many wonders and signs were done...praising God and having favor with all the people. And the Lord added to the church daily those who were being saved."

MISSION GREECE | 3

The mission to Greece was a long time in planning.

Long before August of 1973, there was a plan to take young people to Greece for ministry.

While I was training our young people in the principles of the gospel, I thought it was important to present them with an opportunity to live out those principles, and in the process involve themselves in evangelism. And, that's how the mission to Greece was born.

The young people, all of them in their teens, had never been to Greece, and for me it was the first time I was to return to the land of my birth since I came to the United States.

Thus, I started an intensive training in informing them about Greece, how the people are different in customs and experience, and how we could prepare ourselves in order to have a successful ministry.

There was also a flurry of activities initiated in order for those who would participate to obtain funds to cover their expenses. We had to secure permits from stores where we could have bake sales, arrange and spend some money in order to have car washes and so on. All these activities were done in the space of one year. The young people responded to all of these duties with much enthusiasm and great stamina.

Finally, those who were able to go to the mission, came from the families of our Church: Daniel & Effie Kalem, Gus & Helen Argyropoulos, Arthur & Voula Babbes, Gust and Marina Lillas from Seattle, and a friend of one of the participants named Valerie as also a young woman from Australia named Kathy. Theo also joined us in Greece and proved to be a great coordinator and a travel advisor.

The time came. August 1973. The whole month of August, we moved all over Greece and the island of Crete. We visited churches, camps and wherever they wanted us. We sung Greek Youth songs, new songs which were popular in the US but not in Greece, and I preached evangelistic messages.

We had rented a mini van that presented us with all kinds of problems. On a road trip to Thessaloniki, we were traveling on a mountainous road with nothing around us, when two of our tires went flat. We parked the van off the road, and we were looking for someone who would stop to help us.

One in particular, a Belgian man telling from the license plates on his car, stopped a little further down the road to help, and I tried to strike a conversation with him.

I asked him, Do you speak English, to which he said no. Parlez vous Francais? I asked again. Again, he said no... Then he asked me, Sprechen Sie Deutsch? My turn now to respond, nein. Again, he asked me, Hablas Espanol? At the moment I remember Valerie spoke Spanish, turn around and yelled to Theo in Greek, "Tell Valerie to come over right away". And the man from the car asked "Are you Greeks too, guys?" He then told us that he was himself Greek, and a resident of Belgium. This kind man then helped us take the tires to the next town, where we found a service station able to help us continue our trip north.

I remember vividly a meeting we held at the church in the city of Katerini south of Thessaloniki. The young people sung several songs, and then came my time to preach. At the end of my preaching, I gave an invitation for anyone to come forward for salvation or any other need.

There were people who responded, and among them was a young man in his teens who came forward to give his heart to Jesus. He was moved he said by our young people singing so enthusiastically, been himself a musician. Now, this young man is the pastor of that church in Katerini and the President of the Synod of our churches in Greece. Praise the Lord!

I remember a young lady in her teens named Sofie who attended one of our youth camp meetings we ministered to in the city of Kalamos not far from Athens. She told me, "I see the women in your group, who are not much older than we team leaders are. They are so dedicated to the Lord, they sing and pray with all their heart and they preach their faith boldly. Also, we see they are dressed in a contemporary and attractive fashion. They bring a new way of contact to us Christian girls in Greece. So, if we are to evangelize our young contemporaries, we need to be transformed to worthy missionaries. Not only to dedicate ourselves to the Lord completely but to also be dressed in an acceptable way."

"Go therefore and make disciples of all the nations, baptizing them in the name of the Father and of the Son and of the Holy Spirit. Teaching them to observe all that I commanded you; and lo, I am with you always, even to the end of the age."
(Matthew 28:19-20)

and also to the Greeks

GREEK HOUR OF HOPE BROADCAST | 4

Having my first experience with radio in Greece, I was given a new commission by the Lord while in college to reach the Greeks of America with the Gospel of Jesus Christ using this medium.

The time had come to preach Jesus Christ through radio. It was at the end of 1973.

Two women members of the Greek Assembly would tell me every time they saw me, "Pastor, you should go on radio." These were Mrs. Jessie McClain and Mrs. Fay Masterson. Sunday after Sunday they would repeat the same "Pastor, you should go on radio." So, finally, I decided to put words into action.

I went to the offices of the largest Christian radio station KFAX on Pine Street in San Francisco, to see the manager and talk to him about a Greek Christian radio program. I asked that it would be best if it will follow another Greek program. There was another Greek program on the station already and I asked if mine could come after this so that the station will serve better their Greek audience. The manager agreed and told me I can have it for $25 a week. I gave the manager a time in the future I would like to start and will get back to him.

I returned knowing that I will be committing the Church to $1,300 a year, a large amount for our Church at that time.

I prayed about the funds that were needed. I remember telling the Lord that I will start if I had half of that amount on hand, and will take it as His will. So, I told our people that I would start radio broadcasts in Greek over KFAX, and I needed their support in the next three months before I start.

Week after week and Sunday after Sunday, we were praying for the Lord to provide the funds for the radio. But hardly anyone was giving to the new project. Only our retired pastor Rev. George Samatzis, who had the faith to see souls come to Christ, gave one hundred dollars. This gift toward the radio together with some smaller donations brought the amount to $150.

The project was dead, for all practical purposes, for no other gifts were coming in. And, I had kept it a secret what I had agreed with the Lord about starting if I had half the funds needed for six months in advance.

It seemed that we could not start the radio program on the time we had agreed with the station manager. And the encouragement I received from the two women members had turned now into discouragement. But on the last Sunday, I receive an envelope containing $500 from an old, beloved lady who lived alone and was on social security to live on, Mrs. Sofia Krouscas. So, radio started on time, on God's timing, October 4, 1974, on my twenty ninth birthday by the way, and on God's having provided the funds needed.

Then I sought the help of my classmate from Bethany College, Stan Lindvall, who was working on another Christian station in San Carlos. I would go there to meet him and to learn from him how to make my first broadcasts. We were using then reel-to-reel tapes and we had to splice them and put them together. It was fun!

Through the more than 45 years of radio ministry, we have used reel-to-reel tapes, cassettes and finally CDs. I was able to broadcast on various series, like the Embrace of God, Books of the Bible, as also bilingual programs like The Twelve Gods, Greek Temples, America's Parthenon and Without Christmas. I also prepared other programs, as The Death of the Drachma, Onesiphorus the Merciful, The Prayer of Jabez with Rev. Robert Creel, and one with Dr. Fotios Litsas about loneliness. I also had invited guest speakers on as Dr. Emmanuel Deligiannis, Rev. Georgia Zakedis and many others. The broadcast has always to do with contemporary issues analyzed through God's Word.

My brother Theo became my announcer, we used music and technical assistance by George Argyropoulos and many other sources, and our secretary Julie Kalem prepared the tapes and then mailed them to the various stations. She also would respond to request we received for Bibles and other help.

The results were phenomenal. People would listen faithfully and grow in the Lord. Others would be saved around the world, and many would ask taped programs to be sent to them - for themselves, or for loved ones who were near death to listen and be comforted.

One example in particular stands out in the history of our radio ministry.

In the beginning, I received a letter after a program I presented about Christmas. The letter went like this: "Dear Speaker, if I was close to you, I would have embraced you and kissed you. My name is Gus and I am a 90-year-old man. I used to be a bad boy, I became a bad man, and I am now bad old man. I went to church and did everything the priest told me, but I don't have peace in my heart. Please, tell me how to become a good Christian, and if I can, I would try to do it." Signed, Gus from San Francisco.

I answered immediately telling the listener that I will answer his question on the next program which will be for him.

On the next program, I basically said that you don't have to do anything to be saved, because Jesus Christ did everything needed for you by taking your place on the cross and paying the debt of your sin. Now, the only thing God required of you is to believe in your heart that Christ was born as a man, died for your sins, and rose from the dead, to repent of your sins, and to receive Him in your heart.

Then I received a second letter from the listener, that went like this:

"Mr. Vourliotis, Thank you very much for explaining the Bible to me. I did as you said, I opened my heart to Jesus and believed in Him who died for me on the cross, I repented of my sins, and now I have peace in my heart and I can sleep at night for the first time in my life. Now, I have the joy of the Lord and I know I will go to heaven to be with Christ my savior." Two years later, Gus went to meet the Lord he loved and he found so late in his life.

But the whole story of Gus' life revealed how much God loved him. Earlier in his life, Gus was an enemy of Christ. People from our Church would go on Sunday afternoons to San Francisco into Greek Town, to witness to Greeks who will congregate there. And, Gus was always there to antagonize them, taking their tracts and Bibles and throwing them away, saying things that hurt them, and making their service to their Lord so difficult. But God had a plan for him also, to come to know him, and to be saved because God loved him so much that He gave His only Son for him who believed in Him.

Stories like Gus's and many others, encourage us to continue serving Christ, and proclaiming his love through radio. The Greek Hour of Hope which originated more than 45 years ago on one station in

Evangelizing Hope

the San Francisco Bay Area, now has grown to broadcast the good news of the gospel over many regular and internet stations in three continents, in North America, Australia and Europe, and an internet station in Athens, Greece.

And there are people who want Greeks to be saved who send in their support month after month. I thank God for another Dr. Gus, also from California, who had a special interest in broadcasting in Florida, the area of Tampa, that he was underwriting the entire cost of the station there for many years until he went to be with the Lord he served through the ministry of giving.

One day we will receive of the Lord rewards, that will be proportional to what we did for Him, if we proclaimed the gospel, if we prayed for a lifesaving project, if we gave money for it, and if we prepared the tapes and responded to requests. But at the end, we will all glorify Jesus for loving us and let us be his hand extended to a needy world.

Digitizing our radio broadcasts for safekeeping was our desire for the past few years. We brought this need to the Lord our provider in prayer and waited. Some twelve months ago someone called-in and expressed the same desire. Immediately after him another person with no connection to each other offered to underwrite the cost of digitizing all our 45-plus years radio broadcasts.

We praised God and then we did a good market search from coast to coast, to locate the best company to do the job for us. We were astonished to find out that the best and most economical company was just next door. Yes, in Oakland, California, less than 10 miles close to us. So, over the last twelve months, this expert company has been digitizing all the broadcasts; tapes, reel-to-reel, cassettes, CDs, all of them and the job is wonderful!

Soon the whole job will be complete. Our hope is that the next generation will continue to preach the gospel through them, and even now go on the internet and on radio stations, that our co-laborers will want to fund and continue this soul saving ministry.

"I shall run the course of your commandments, for you shall enlarge my heart."
Psalm 119:32

"He sends out His command to the earth; His word runs very swiftly."
Psalm 147:15.

THE CIRCLE OF MISSIONS | 5

In the 1920's there was revival in the San Francisco Bay Area.

A young Greek man was working on the ship-lines making runs between Oakland and San Francisco. Someone invited this young man to Glad Tidings Temple in San Francisco where revival services were going on. At a service where the Holy Spirit was moving, the young man was drawn to God and he received the call to missions. So, he enrolled in the Bible School to better prepare himself for the work the Lord had called him.

He, then, became involved in the Greek work that was flourishing in San Francisco and then in Oakland. It didn't take long for Harry Mamalis to be looking forward to the day he will go to his native land and preach the gospel there.

So, in the late 1920's, Harry Mamalis and Eddy Dictos departed as missionaries to Greece. While Eddy Dictos went to the northern part of Greece, Harry Mamalis went to Athens to visit a family he was given the name and address by a distant relative in California. He knocked at the door, and a 16-year-old girl named Rosa, the adopted daughter of the family, answered the door and welcomed the American missionary to their home.

The Deligiannis family at that address were very happy to receive Harry Mamalis and to hear news from the distant relative. But they were happier when Rev. Mamalis gave them the message he was bringing from God. He was given an opportunity to teach them the good news from the Word of the Lord and young Rosa was the first to respond to the message, to accept the Lord as her savior and to be baptized with the Holy Spirit. She was Harry Mamalis' first spiritual fruit in Athens. Rosa's adopted mother used to attend the First Presbyterian Church of Athens but she was a back-slider at that time. She then renewed her commitment to God and received the baptism in the Holy Spirit. So, Rosa and her mother were the first members of the Church that was started in that house in Athens.

Rosa who was born on the Greek island of Tenos, lost her father at 4 years of age and her mother at 8. So, she stopped going to school because she was brought by her much older brother Peter to Athens and consequently was adopted by the prominent Deligiannis family who lived in a very good neighborhood in the city center.

After the initial service at their home with Harry Mamalis, Rosa, who was then full of the Holy Spirit, followed faithfully the services and the Lord worked in her heart. She was so dedicated to the Lord that she had a vision of Christ (Acts 2:17). And she's given the gift of an evangelist and told everyone in sight how much the Lord loved them, and how to accept him in their heart. Many in the neighborhood heard the gospel from Rosa and many are in heaven today because of her.

A year later the Lord spoke to her to go into "the highways and hedges" and preach the gospel. However, considering herself inadequate to accept the call of the Lord as she had completed only the second grade of grammar school, she made an agreement with Him that her children will answer His call instead. And, when she got married 12 years later and had four sons, she instructed them all to walk with the Lord as special as they were, and prayed for them constantly.

Sure enough, all of her four sons, made their choice to dedicate their lives to Jesus and to serve the Lord. Two of them who are surviving are still serving the Lord today. One of the sons, who followed her example of been a person of prayer and an evangelist, was called of God inside their home to go teach and preach the gospel when he was exactly at the age God had called his mother, at 16 years of age.

After he studied in Europe, he came to the US to continue his studies. Toward the end of his studies in Santa Cruz, the Lord directed him, not to the Los Angeles Greek Apostolic church, or somewhere else, but to pastor the Greek Assembly in Oakland of all places, where Harry Mamalis started his walk with God, the missionary who established that church in Athens. That young man is the one who writes this book!

As I was first introduced to the Greek Assembly in Oakland, it was another pastor who preceded me there, Harry Mamalis' son Theophilos, who was happy to welcome me there, and gave me the first advice. And, then, after accepting their invitation to be their pastor, I found Harry Mamalis himself in that Church, retired but still active in ministry for His Lord.

He lived in an assisted living home not far from the church, and every day you would find him at a busy corner of a popular supermarket on Fruitvale Avenue, at the Dimond District area in East Oakland, where he would give out tracts, and talk to people about God's love to them and pray with them, until he couldn't do it any longer.

I am sorry I was in Greece preaching when this great man of God and missionary to the Greeks died and could not minister at his funeral. But I was honored to be present at Mrs. Mamalis' funeral and eulogized her a few years later.

So, missions sometimes make a complete circle. Rev. Harry Mamalis was sent by God from Northern California to Greece to bring the good news of the gospel to my Mother Rosa in Athens, and then God directed my steps, Rosa's third son, to come to Oakland, back to where this pioneer missionary to the Greeks found the Lord and was called to go to Greece, with the call and the vision remaining the same: evangelizing the Greeks.

Doesn't God have a sense of humor? Or, He does His work with a purpose and a program, that is the Holy Spirit's guiding and moving. He is the Lord of the harvest and those who care for the harvest let their lives be consumed by the cares of the harvest.

"For I am mindful of the sincere faith within you (Timothy, my beloved son), which first dwelt in your.... mother Eunice, and I am sure that it is in you as well.... For God has not given us the spirit of fear, but of power and love and of a sound mind." 2 Timothy 1:5-7

GOD WANTS ALL TO BE SAVED | 6

"God is not slow about his promise," says 2 Peter 3:9. God promised to end history of the ungodly men with judgment. But God is not unfaithful to His promise. He is patient. He extends the time of grace so that men have every opportunity to get saved.

In Isaiah 61:2, we read of the year of the Lord's favor and the day of His vengeance. He means that God extends His longsuffering 1000 years and condenses His judgement to one day. He waited 120 years before He sent the Flood. Now He is waiting several thousand years before destroying the world with fire. Thus, he continues in 2 Peter 3:9, "The Lord is longsuffering toward us, not willing that any should perish, but that all should come to repentance." (2 Peter 3:9)

There were people in our ministry, whom God saved the last moment.

There were two men, who were friends for years in drinking together. They were both associated with our church people who prayed for them and cared for their physical needs.

One was Robert. The other, named Lee, liked to live like a bum although he had a good job and lots of money.

They have now died, and I trust they are in heaven with the Lord.

On January 27, 2021, we received a call from a local hospital that Lee was there and had not much hope of coming out alive. So, immediately, I decided to pay him a visit with Julie, our secretary, who was related to him.

There were a lot of details we had to go through to make sure we can make the visit and even got the advice of a nurse and his wife who attend our church, because of Covid-19.

Finally, we went to the hospital, where the staff were waiting for us, and took us right away to the patient in the intensive care unit.

Evangelizing Hope

I was with Lee for about fifteen minutes, at which time I shared the love of God with him and prayed for him to accept the Lord.

We left the hospital not knowing what will happen next, but they called us later to tell us that Lee had died two and half hours later.

Now, Robert who was Lee's drinking bud, had ended up in a nursing home on Fruitvale Avenue near our Church several years earlier.

One day I had a strong urging in my heart to go visit him and talk to him about his salvation.

So, I got in my car and went to the nursing home. I was there at about 11 in the morning.

They brought Robert in the guest area. Thank God we were there alone. The long-term drinking problem had affected his face that it looked as something was missing. I read from the Word of God, and prayed leading him to accept the Lord as his savior, as I held his hand.

I left, and the urgency I felt in my heart was lifted. A peace came over me, knowing that God was in control.

The people at the nursing home called to tell me that Robert had died a few hours later on the same day I visited him.

There was also David, who was brought to our Church by our associates at the time Rev. Danny and Berta Martinez.

David was born in Chicago on April 3, 1960 and soon after his birth was abandoned by his mother and left for his grandmother to raise him. While in his late teens, David had moved to the San Francisco Bay Area where he was involved in a life of drugs.

But, in God's mercy, he was introduced to Teen Challenge, an organization that minister to persons addicted to drugs and alcohol, and graduated from the program in 1982. Through Teen Challenge, he got acquainted with Danny and Berta Martinez who became his friends, and then brought him to our Church in 1984.

I remember, I was preaching on that Sunday on the love of God, and interpreted myself from English into Greek for the benefit of all the Greek-speaking believers attending. David thought that I was speaking in tongues and interpreted in English, and rushed forward to rededicate his life to Christ.

David became a loyal member of our church, attending all our services and activities.

He took the Berean University courses through the Greek Center for Biblical Studies, and successfully completed the course "Marriage and Family," in the Spring of 1999.

Through his 18-year association with the Greek Assembly, David who was loved by all, offered his cheerful service in various areas of ministry, for he loved God with all his heart, and for sometime he assisted Rev. Harry Leid, an Assemblies of God minister and missionary, at the Oakland Full Gospel Mission.

On Thursday, August 8, 2002, the Lord called David to his heavenly home, as he passed away at the Summit Hospital at 6:08 pm.

Jesus saved the sinner on the cross, saying to him, "today you shall be with Me in Paradise."

"For God so loved the world, that He gave His only begotten Son, that whosoever believeth in Him should not perish, but have everlasting life." (John 3:16) and also to the Greeks

THE PROPHETIC LEADING | 7

Isaiah 48:17 says, "Thus, says the Lord, your redeemer, the Holy One of Israel: 'I am the Lord your God......Who leads you in the way you should go.'"

In the book of Acts, we see the Lord leading the early believers through the gift of prophecy.

Of the seven chosen in chapter 6 of Acts, Steven was mentioned first who became the first martyr. The second to be mentioned was Philip, a mighty evangelist.

When persecution arose, Philip went to Samaria where He preached with signs following. There, we read, "For unclean spirits, crying with loud voices, came out of many ...and that were lame, were healed. And there was great joy in that city." (Acts 8:7-8)

Next, we read that God spoke to Philip through an angel "Arise, and go toward the south to the way that goes down from Jerusalem to Gaza, which is desert. So, he arose and went. And behold, a man of Ethiopia, a eunuch, of great authority under Candace, the queen of the Ethiopians, who had charge of all her treasury; and had come to Jerusalem to worship, was returning. And sitting in his chariot, he was reading Isaiah the prophet. Then the Spirit said to Philip, 'Go near and overtake this chariot. So, Philip ran to him, and heard him reading Isaiah, and said, "Do you understand what you are reading? And he said, 'How can I, unless someone guides me?" And he asked Philip to come up and sit with him." (Acts 8:26-31)

Later, we see the Ethiopian saying, "I believe that Jesus Christ is the Son of God." After Philip baptized him, when they came up out of the water, the Spirit of the Lord caught Philip away, so that the eunuch saw him no more, and he went on his way rejoicing. But Philip was found at Azotus. And passing through, he preached in all the cities till he came to Caesarea." (Acts 8:37-40)

Then, we find Philip at his home in Caesarea when Paul visited him. We read in 21:8, "On the next day we departed and came to Caesarea, (Luke is speaking) and entered the house of Philip the evangelist, who was one of the seven, we stayed with him. Now this man had four virgin daughters who prophesied."

"And as we stayed many days, a certain prophet named Agabus came down from Judea. When he had come to us, he took Paul's belt, bound his own hands and feet, and said, Thus, says the Holy Spirit, so shall the Jews at Jerusalem bind the man who owns this belt, and deliver him into the hands on the Gentiles."

The four young women, daughters of Philip, anointed by the Spirit, expounded the truth, for Revelation 19:10 says, "The testimony of Jesus is the spirit of prophecy." They could also speak of things to happen, under certain circumstances, with the ability to foretell.

Agabus and others foretold how Paul will suffer at Jerusalem (Acts 21:10-11), and that there would be a great famine in the land (Acts 11:27).

In the 1970s, the Holy Spirit was moving among the Catholic Church and the Classical Evangelical

Churches, and many were exposed to the Spirit's fullness.

It was at that time the Lord chose to give me "the third great call of God."

We had a guest from Greece, and I decided to take him in a large meeting where a minister with a prophetic ministry was scheduled who was known for giving prophetic messages based on Scripture.

We found two seats in the back of the great hall where there should have been 1000 people. And, the minister was ready as we all were looking at him.

Then, while seated, he pointed to five or seven people he wanted to minister to, to come up to the platform. Among them he called also me.

I went up, with the others, and I remember what happened like it was yesterday.

He gave me a message on encouragement, telling me to walk with confidence for God will enlarge my ministry to the Greeks and increase it. And he used the passage from Isaiah 54:2-4

"Enlarge the place of your tent, and let them stretch out the curtains of your dwellings; Do not spare; Lengthen the cords, and strengthen your stakes. For you shall extend to the right and to the left...."

I received this message with reverence. But I was asking God for a confirmation of that which the minister has said will be so. I was in prayer about it, for I believe the Lord takes pleasure when His people ask for His confirmation.

The Lord used an unusual way to confirm what I had heard at one of our Friday Prayer meetings.

The meeting was at Brother & Sister George & Georgia Zakides house in Newark, California. I had asked the people to kneel in prayer, after a short teaching.

Sister Georgia had invited two ladies. I didn't know who they were, but while we were kneeling and praying, these two women came near me and very silently they asked if they could pray over me. I said go ahead. These two women, who were prophetesses, they started to prophecy over me, telling me the same exact message I had heard from the famous prophet, and confirming what The Holy Spirit had already said.

and also to the Greeks

There was another type of confirmation that followed.

Immediately, I had invitations to go minister to Greek groups from the West Coast of the United States to Arizona, New Mexico, Colorado and other states, and to place our broadcast on new stations.

First, I was invited to go to Seattle, then Portland was quickly added. Then, I received a call from Tom and Paula Mentis to visit Arizona and minister to a group of believers who had left their Church and were seeking more of the Spirit of God in their lives.

Then, came New Mexico with Evan & Mary Marmarelis, and Colorado followed. I remember visiting 34 Greek restaurants in Denver with the greatest Greek evangelist of our day, Dimitri Kountouris. He was also responsible for placing our Greek broadcast on a Christian Radio Station in Denver.

Then, Thomas Siapkaris introduced our program on a radio station in Texas, and a sister in the Lord Gwen Harris, introduced our radio program in North Carolina.

Sometimes, I would go alone by plane or with a car gifted by Rev. Dula Xinos of Seattle with my brother

Theo. Then, we would cross states and hundreds upon hundreds of miles, taking with us young people who had a heart for the lost.

While all these advances were achieved for the gospel, there were also challenges.

There was a priest who traveled some 500 miles in the East Coast to tell the manager of a radio station, a born-again believer, not to have our program on for we were preaching lies. On the return trip, he had an accident and ended-up in a hospital.

In the Mid-West, the priest told his people on Sunday that there was going to be a new Greek broadcast on the Christian radio station and admonished them not to listen to it. Of course, their curiosity made them listen. A couple invited me in their house and offered me "raki," a kind of strong alcohol spirit they made themselves. I offered them a message from the Spirit of God.

In the West Coast, a prominent church leader sent out letters and went on radio to vehemently oppose our soul saving message. He was not at all polite in naming us names, and it was sad to read and hear his rebuke as he scolded us to his people and the radio audience, saying among other false accusations, "Beware of ravening wolves who are dressed in sheep's clothing."

And we were praying like the early believers did, for God to hear their accusations against us. Somehow, he was fired from his position a few months later and until the end he never found out the reason. For leaders in his position in his church don't get fired. They carry on their title and position till they die.

In I Corinthians 14:1 says, "Pursue love, and desire spiritual gifts, but especially that you may prophesy." And, later, in verse 3, "But he who prophesies speaks edification and exhortation and comfort to men."

While all preaching is not prophecy, but anointed preaching could be.

So, pray and seek the ministry of prophecy in order to edify the Church.

ENDORSEMENTS

With this morning mail I received your book AND ALSO TO THE GREEKS. My interest in the Greeks, Greek ministry, as well as in your own ministry, caused me to begin reading it immediately.

I wish I had known some of these things about you and your family years ago. We remember sharing a meal in your parent's home more than fifty years ago. They were extremely hospitable... And, we have appreciated the opportunities we have had through the years to be in fellowship with you.

I was reading in Colossians this morning that the Apostle Paul established his credentials with the saints there by telling them that he was an apostle "by the will of God." You have certainly proven yourself to be an apostle by the will of God to the beautiful Greek People. We salute you and hold you in our prayers.

DR. EVERETT STENHOUSE, Idaho

I enjoyed learning some of the details of your early life and journey to hear, answer and fulfill the call of God. I'm struck with the vision God gave you of the path ahead you would travel.

So happy our paths crossed. Congratulations on a long and fruitful ministry. Continue until He calls us to the final step of the way! I will meet you at a Heavenly Hellenic taverna!

REV. GEORGE A GIANOPULOS, North Carolina

It is such a blessing to see how the Lord led your every step.

MRS. META BLANTON, Florida

It is truly one miracle after another of how God puts us in places where we'll flow with Him.

REV. PAULA MENTIS, Arizona

I read your book and I found it to be inspiring, learning how God intervened in your life to direct you in His calling for you.

MS EFFIE VLAHAKIS, Southern California

I really enjoyed reading your book and it was such an inspiration and encouragement. I cannot tell you how much at this time I needed to read and hear about personal faith and how God cares and guides.

It confirmed again how much he does understand our needs and what is best. It is not always easy to see or understand but your testimony and the great adventures you have lived are example of His hand.

Thank you for sharing and much love to you. I had NO idea you spoke French!

NICK COKAS, San Francisco, CA

I received your book and finished reading this morning. It was a blessing and inspiration and challenge. I hope you are writing a sequel. God has directed your footsteps and opened miraculous doors for your ministry. It has been a blessing to know you and visit Greece on a mission trip, as well as the retreat at Lake Tahoe, and to attend the Greek Assembly of God many times through the years.

MRS LINDA POUNCE, Alabama

www.ingramcontent.com/pod-product-compliance
Lightning Source LLC
Chambersburg PA
CBHW032059040426
42449CB00007B/1144